BREATH OF A
FALLEN
ANGEL

Damaris Chanza

AOS Publishing, 2024

ISBN: 978-1-998662-05-0

Cover Design: Meredith Lindsay

Visit AOS Publishing's website:
www.aospublishing.com

To women everywhere,

for your endurance and bravery for surviving
on this earth with a vagina.

This book contains sensitive material relating to: domestic violence trauma abuse sex murder and possibly more that could be triggering. Please take care of yourself and take a step back if you need to. Remember that your mental and emotional health are always a priority.

Table of Contents

To Begin

Just a simple girl,
riddled with ambition,
destined to conquer the world,
until a man strips away her inhibitions.

She's been here before,
time and time again,
charmed by the love lore,
only to be heartbroken.

But, this time she stays,
convinced something can change,
until she too starts to play,
and the roles are rearranged.

Soon a hostage to her own brain,
strangled by the grasp of love and hate.
Stability and commitment, she craved,
but, immorality is all he could demonstrate.

Confused by truth,
enamored by lies,
stifled by couth,
too torn to say goodbye.

With wavering strength,
grown from fights past,
will come a moment so tense,
she'll be aghast.

OK, enough of that, let's rewind,
to when summer and autumn blend.
With the scene set, keep in mind;
if it's not okay, it's not the end.

Special

You're such a cute young thing,
big-eyed and wide-smiled.
You haven't been tortured by what life can bring.
Maybe we should hang for a while.

Short legs and thick thighs;
I'd love to see you on your knees.
I just love to watch you walk by.
Let me touch your body, please!

See? I asked nicely.
We'll take it nice and slow.
Will you fuck me if I'm friendly?
Just a suggestion, let me know.

Like my smile? Find me charming?
Wow, my grip is the circumference of your waist.
I see you're an ocean, why not let me dive in?
Don't worry, baby, I'll just take a little taste.

Wasn't that good?
Now, let me show you great.
Why not treat it like food?
No? That's fine; I'll wait.

You sure?
Maybe, you want a facial.
Come on, baby, don't be a bore,
don't you know you're special?

. . .

I thought so.
You made me feel celestial,
but you put me aside and let me go.
It turns out I was just yesterday's special.

Ending the Cycle

Here I am,
lost again.
In my search for love;
all I've found are duds–
scrubs who marvel at my supposed beauty.

I grow fond,
we build a bond,
then he's gone,
off to another.

One day I'm special.
The next, I'm erased.
A cycle I can't escape.

I wish it played like the greats wrote it.
A glance and a smile;
would be enough to beguile.
I would choose him;
and he would choose me.
No more games to play.

But, I choose wrong,
and before long,
life's a sad song,
again.

Or I leave too quick,
decide he's a dick;
having fallen for another trick.

Despite stories past,
I have this feeling,
the next one will last.

'Til then I'll work,
continue to create.
I just know;
He'll be perfect.
For Him,
I'll wait.

Creating Woman

Art is about the person, the people, the experiences, and situations existing all across the world.
It's about the feelings and the thoughts that pour into something as simple as a dress.
It's not about the simplicity of being woman.
It's about the creation of woman.
It's about how dresses or pants define you as weak or empowered.
It's about how straight hair or curls define you as professional or wild.
It's about how vocabulary changes the status of opinion even if the statement does not change.

Art is about the small intricacies of thought that cannot be expressed with basic language.
It's about how perseverance amidst adversity equals strength but not respect.
It's about how childbearing and entrepreneurship can coexist even if others disagree.
Or maybe it's about working as much and as hard as a man but without equal pay.

Art is about being an artist without the recognition of talent or message.
Art is about the return and redefinition of femininity as our own.

Art

Sometimes it feels lonely;
Sometimes it feels comfortable.
The silence can be deafening and calming.
The soft touch of my blanket sometimes feels like thorns piercing
my thighs.

I can feel trapped.
I can feel free.
The walls close in with little space to breathe and create.
Yet, creativity bursts from the air.

And I, with a blank stare.

The Bar

How can I raise the bar?
Who am I to think I could be a star;
traveling the world for all to see?
They don't want me.
I won't get words of praise.
I'll be lucky if I'm even a phase;
but, I'm not the lucky type.
I'm not one to get lots of hype.

But, wouldn't it be cool?
My books in libraries and schools,
people remembering my name.
I'm not looking for fame;
but, wow, it'd be nice.
Maybe, I do suffice.

How can I raise the bar?
Doesn't matter,
I'd probably never make it that far.

Him

What's his name?
I forgot.
I was too distracted once that silky voice escaped his lips.
I don't know how I managed to be so tame.
His smile sparked a trance I couldn't resist,
like Cupid's arrow took its aim.

And those eyes,
they glisten like the sea in the moonlight.
I couldn't look away.
You might call it love at first sight,
but I'm blinded by his shine.

From his height;
to the dimple in his cheeks,
everything was so perfect.
From the eloquent way that he speaks;
to the way his words infect;
my heart. I can't believe;
he would choose me.

Stupid

That smirk drives me wild.

Take a breath,
don't say something stupid;
can't have you thinking I'm dim;
need to smile brighter and laugh louder,
but not too bright or too loud.
Can't help feeling like you might think I'm too much;
or maybe not enough?
Want to be perfect;
need to be perfect.
What's perfect, anyway?
You.
Waiting for you to notice me.
Have to make a great impression.
Slowly approaching your grace.
Take a breath;
and don't say anything stupid.

Smudged

Cheeks match my cherry lips;
Eyes locked;
Hands around my waist;
Inching me closer;
Lust in your eyes;
Failing to hide my smile;
Nose to nose;
Feeling your breath on mine;
Eyes closed;
Lipstick smudging;
Bodies melting into one another;
Hearts thumping like church bells;
Tied the knot with our tongues;
Lungs craving air;
Craving each other;
Feeling bliss in this kiss.

Love

Leave your clothes behind;
I want to feel your skin on mine;
Feel our bodies intertwine;
You feel so sublime;
We should do this all the time;
Sweat making our bodies shine;
Damn! You're in your prime;
Reaching for the top, ring that chime;
Baby, I'm up for the climb;
Making me lose my mind;
Feels like paradise in this sin, this crime;
Forget everything I'm blind;
Love now clearly defined;
Our souls forever combined. . .

Those Three Words

If I could lock eyes with you just once more;
If my fingertips could graze along the side of your cheek;
If my lips could create the right shape;
If my tongue could dance as beautifully as we do in my dreams;
And if I could inhale just the right amount of air;
Maybe I could formulate those three words loud enough for you
to hear.

Louder

Surrounded by white noise,
I venture into the light.
Isolated from my own kind,
I want to speak,
have you hear my voice,
but, I don't make a sound.
I'm too scared.
Burdened with silence,
guess, I'll have to hide my frown.

6AM

Flat on my back with my feet hanging off the edge, I lay in bed.
My eyes closed in unfulfilled slumber,
I heard a noise, but I'm not sure what you said.
Still, it was your voice,
all smooth and golden.
I rustled in my sheets,
waived my arm over to place my hand on your chest,
a movement I've made plenty of times before;
times when we were at our best.
Instead, I hit a wall.
Naked and cold, I opened my eyes.
I lay alone.
How bold of me to assume you'd be home.

I Do

Here I am tonight;
walking in the twilight;
draped in white,
lovely to be,
marching hesitantly,
with fleeting serenity;
up to thee.

Guided by faith,
accepting your scathe,
with no trace;
of blessings,
but I'm just obsessing.

With this ring,
I give this love a real chance.
I give no other man a second glance,
and vow to shower you in romance.

Let this ring;
be a symbol of my love for you,
and your love for me, too.
Now, I say I do.

Awake

You ever think about how nothing is permanent?
How not even the shining sun in the sky is guaranteed?
After all the clouds hide it away all the time.

You ever think about how everything is broken?
From the tree you call a desk to the hidden earth you call a road;
whether cut or trimmed it's not in its true state anymore.

You ever think about the relativity of new?
New job, old cycle, new clothes, old laundry, new car, old
destinations;
New doesn't even mean new anymore.

You ever think about how your brain won't shut off at night?
How the silence screams truths in your ears?
It shouts and shouts delaying your burdensome slumber.

Yeah,
Me neither.

Blindsided

Caught up in the possibility of us;
Thinking you were a divine gift from above.
Lost in your light so bright;
It blinded me to the truth.
It blinded me from the real you.

Your Demon

Met him yesterday;
Your Hyde;
broke out of his cage.
Blindsided.

Saw his face;
Your Lucifer,
unleashed his rage.
He wanted me to suffer.

Felt his talon;
Your demon's,
handprint on my face.
How the mighty have fallen.

Walking With My Eyes Closed

Eyes closed,
blankets wrapped,
messy hair and lips chapped.
Suddenly,
alarm snapped.

Wake up,
give my eyes a rub,
stay down, feel like giving up.
Have to go fill my coffee cup.
Eventually,
I'm standing up.

Glasses on, then, go pee;
Eyes open but can't see.
Damn, hit my knee.
Thankfully,
I have my coffee.

No time to sit;
Have to pick a fit;
Eyes feeling heavy, can't give a shit.
Quickly,
dressed to deal with all of it.

Shoes on;
Hair brushed and chap-stick on;
Eyes drowsy, need to move on.
Foolishly,
waiting for my eyes to turn on.

Daydreams

There once was a time,
when your demon was still hidden,
locked away in your internal hell,
unknown to our love.
When your presence cast a spell,
and your kiss bloomed roses,
and your sex cured droughts;
A time when your words rubbed my edges to curves.
Like magic,
your touch spread warmth throughout my body,
and your charm rivaled princes of lore.

It was beautiful.
Inseparable were we;
Believed to be,
walking on clouds;
Dancing into the sunset;
Pure fantasy out of my dreams.

But darkness creeped in;
Creating a villain;
Set on breaking my heart;
Cursing our love sour;
Poisoning my days,
into nightmares.

But it happened;
True or not;
There was a time,
when we loved like a fairytale.
Now only glimpses of memories far far away;
Gone as they may be,
I still walk with Him in my daydreams.

I Saw

You picked me.
You chose me.
So who is she?

I saw the charge,
for the roses,
that weren't for me.

I saw the stain,
on your collar,
in a shade my lips did not leave.

I saw your schedule,
go from nine to five,
to later than I should believe.

I saw your attitude,
grow farther,
than I thought could be achieved.

I see your flesh,
less and less,
naked between our sheets.

I saw the messages.
I have the proof.
So I ask again;
Who is she?

Anyway

I know I'm crazy,
But, can you love me anyway?

When I ask you about your day and you push me away,
I know I'm nosy,
But, can you love me anyway?

When I ask you to do the dishes after I made dinner,
I know I'm lazy,
But, can you love me anyway?

When I ask to go out with my friends and not with you,
I know I'm selfish,
But, can you love me anyway?

When I ask you about her,
I know I'm jealous,
But, can you love me anyway?

I know I'm crazy,
But, please love me anyway!

I Love You

I love you.
Is that so hard to say?
Monosyllabic words,
in a simple sentence.
You've said it before.
Was I love you,
just a broken promise,
ripped at the seams,
when you slept in her sheets?
Is your love that hard to share?
You've shared it with me before;
When our bodies intertwined,
and our vows were spoken,
Love was there.
So say it aloud.
I love you.
Unless . . .

Sinking

Feeling gravity's touch on my shoulders;
Spine following the curve of my frown;
Few words escaping my cherry-stained lips,
whispered so no one can hear,
how vicious my conscience is.
Smile lost in the sea of intrusive thoughts;
Stuck in the eye of the storm pouring rain down bruised cheeks;
Sunshine and rainbows just out of reach;
Diving deeper only causes more pain;
Fighting it only causes more pain;
How do I fight my own voice,
my own thoughts,
like a siren forcing me to succumb?
Sonically familiar but unrecognizable as my own.
Language echoing yours;
These are not my words;
Sinister and cruel?
That is not me;
That is not who I am;
So why are my thoughts telling me otherwise?

The In-Between

What do you do in the in-between?
When the anger boils inside,
but only at a simmer,
yet somehow it overflows,
with teardrops spilling down your cheeks?
What do you do in that blur?
When the tears swell in your eyes,
to put out the burning fire in your soul?
How do you swim to survive when you can't see your
destination?
Blind with rage,
while drowning in sorrow.
Do you forgive and forget or plot your revenge?

Halfway

Why throw it in my face?
Words both vile and tender,
spoken in the same breath.
"You beautiful dumbass."
It's difficult enough to form the words I want to say,
without you spewing venom in my mind,
telling me about my lack.
My lack of worth,
Intelligence,
Knowledge,
Experience,
Success.
My lack of words.

But, I can meet you halfway.

With me you'd be effaced;
Spit words just as nasty and gentle;
All in the same breath.
"You charming imbecile."
I can yell twice as loud, blocking the words you want to say.
Always planting doubt in your mind.
Telling you about your lack.
Your lack of worth,
Intelligence,
Knowledge,
Experience,
Success.
Your lack of purpose.

You don't want me to meet you halfway.

A Man's Brilliance

Just filled with a man's brilliance;
Bound to live a futile existence;
Bound to the idea of excellence;
Just as your grip bounds me to you;

Just filled with your brilliance;
Your love is my sentence;
Shackled by your sparing repentance;
Verdicts delivered by strikes leaving my skin blue;

Just filled with a woman's brilliance;
My body available for your convenience;
My heart aches for your distance;
Time to speak some truth;

This woman's brilliance is no match for this man's persistence.
This woman's resilience is no match for this man's impatience.
This woman's coexistence with this man may cause her
disappearance.

This woman's ebullience has met interference.

The Edge

Make my skin crawl,
and my blood boil.
Make me listen to your games;
Take everything with a grain.

I'm at the edge;
Barely holding my fists in place;
An eye for an eye,
as they say.
Got me scolding in flames;

The pain is too high;
Share it with me;
I can mirror your demon;
Horns just as sharp;
Spew venom just as dark;
You'll be the one to weaken.

I can do it, too.
Be scared.
You made your own bed.
I can be just as mad,
just as loud,
just as rude.
My spite is just as bad;
My grip just as tight;

Do more;
Get me there;
I'm already at the edge.
You want to play?
Let's play fair.

The Angel & The Demon

Small frame, big heart;
Big brain, small bark;
Frilly and frail;
Petite and polite;
An angel in broad daylight.

Tall build, short fuse;
Short-tempered, tall ruse;
Charming and childish;
Handsome and hollow;
A demon lies in the shadows.

As seen on the streets;
The angel and the demon;
Clear and concise;
One filled with love;
The other with smite;
But what happens behind the scenes?

Brains die as barks rise;
Polite turns to spite;
At dusk, don't forget,
Even angels scowl in the night.

The Price

Loving you is a luxury I can no longer afford;
Debt too great to continue to ignore;
In how many ways do I have to pay?
In puffy eyes and tears cried;
In blood shed and blouses stained red;
In bruises healed and truths concealed;
In lies told and empty vows to uphold;

That spark we thought was magic,
grew into a flame we called passion,
and became a wild fire that couldn't be tamed,
burning everything in sight, our love maimed.

Where did it all go wrong?
Somehow, my prince is really a villain in disguise.
Who have I become,
a twisted perception of love, a guilty vice?
Fairytales did always say that magic came with a price.

Transformed

It happened slowly;
Little did I know your smite was contagious;
With each strike your infectious hatred spread;
It's fight or flight,
but you clipped my wings,
so you've left me with no choice.

I've been reborn;
Transformed into something neither one of us have ever seen
before.
In this new form,
I scratch,
I claw,
I bite.
Make your scars mirror mine,
like cute matching tattoos.

You taught me the recipe for pain,
and good girls make their man a plate.
Attack the eggplant, killing your ego;
Salt your wounds with insults;
Spritz a dash of lemon juice;
Then use the wedge as a chaser,
for the shots of tequila that'll erase your screams.

You stole my heart,
so I'll rip yours apart.
Slash it out of your chest with all my might,
finally relieving all the stress you've placed upon my breast.
Once in my palms, I'll caress it lovingly;
Admire your cold dead heart;
Watch it rot and spoil;

Dangle it in your face as you beg for it back;
Force you to watch when I decide to crush it;
Making it crumble and crack.

Love and hate are no longer defined;
Lines blurred when blood spilled;
Smudged by our delicate footwork;
As we jab, duck, and weave together;
A delicate dance where I'm the one who leads.

Bye

I gave you my heart.
I thought this love was true,
but damn, was I wrong.

I thought we had a good start.
I didn't know it'd turn blue.
Why couldn't we be strong?

You tore our love apart,
tried to stick to my cash like glue.
You need to go back to where you belong.

They told me I should dart,
when your interest in my money grew,
but sweetie, I was ready to tag along.

I should've known the shoe didn't fit from the start.
Like Glass, your lies too good to be true,
but, your voice a melodic song.

Alas our love is tart.
We both know this love is past due.
Our love is not lifelong.
We were once a beautiful piece of art,
but it's time for me to say goodbye to you.
So long. . .

Living the Dream

I am finally free from your abuse.
Tears cried over you are wasted no more.
There is no one left for you to accuse.
I can be the woman I was before.

Despite the roses and the chocolates,
the teddy bears baring apologies,
I know the money came from my wallet.
I'm too smart to fall for your loveless schemes.

Without you I can live my fantasy;
Create the art I was destined to make;
Do all the things you took away from me;
No more living through your pointless heartache.

Everyday I'm reminded of my choice.
I remember the good and the bad;
Think of love I've received from other boys;
Falling so short of the love I once had.

There's a crack in my dream.
Leaving you is not as easy as it seems.

Where Were You?

Where were you,
when his handprint was first tattooed on my cheek?
Where were you,
when his voice rose and mine diminished?
Where were you,
when his words cut wounds only fixed with stitches?
Where were you,
when I listened to you?
I followed you into a world without Him;
Chased you, really;
Ran away from the darkness;
Towards the know;
Towards everything he said no to.
Where were you,
when I needed the support to rebuild?
Where were you,
when my withering hope for freedom was finally killed?

My Mistake

"In sickness and in health"
Is this the sickness?
The vile running through your veins;
The venom spewing from your lips;
Maybe it's just a parasite;
Consuming your kindness;
Eating away at your charm;
Erasing the man I love.
Luckily,
parasites can be removed,
plucked and pruned with flowers and chocolates.

How could I have done this to you?
Leave you in your time of need.
We made vows,
"For better or for worse"
This is worse.
It will get better,
upon my return.

So What?

So, what if I'm fat?
Who even cares about that?
So, maybe my thighs rub and my jeans rip and my skin turns red.

So, what if I'm skinny?
Yeah, I'm a little mini.
So maybe my pants hang loose and my socks slip and my clothes
are too big.

When I lay my head on my bed,
and close my eyes and begin to think,
it's never about the zits or the cellulite,
not about the hair in weird places or my crooked nose,
not even about my messy hair or dark armpits.

In my dreams, I'm perfect,
and when I wake, I feel there must've been a mistake;
in my dreams, I look the exact same as when I'm awake.
So, what could have possibly changed?

Like Me

She's beautiful,
but aren't I?

She twirls in her dress,
and picks flowers on the street.
She hums softly,
and smiles when she speaks.

She holds your hand as I do,
touches your face as I do,
ruffles your hair as I do,
kisses your lips as I do.
She looks at you how I do,
but, I'm the one who said I do.

She doesn't flinch when you wave your hand to move hair from
her face.
She doesn't hide her midriff exposing your handiwork.
She doesn't bite her hands or show signs of anxiety.

Lustrous hair;
Sparkling eyes;
Similar physique;
She looks kind of like me.

She's beautiful,
So why aren't I?

Today

Today,
I feel the monotony,
the weight,
the burden,
of living by your side.

The color drained from my art.
The meaning scraped from my words.
The will escaped from my body.
The thoughts erased from my mind.

Craving a burst of energy,
to ignite my creativity,
to create like I once did.
Now I barely know where to start;
My mind hollow,
and heart split.
Stuck craving better tomorrow's,
and missing my yesterdays,
before you,
when I lived.
But today,
I just survive.

Help

He's not so bad.
No, really, I swear.
So maybe I shed a few tears?
It's not that serious.

He is bad.
Yes, really, I swear.
You should never shed tears.
It is very serious.

It was only once.
It doesn't hurt too bad.
Makeup hides the bruises I had.
He makes me happy.

You don't want it to be more than once.
It should not hurt at all.
Bruises should not exist.
This is not happiness.

It's because he cares.
I can always make more money.
He swears she's just a friend.
I believe him.

This is not what caring looks like.
The money is yours not his.
A friend doesn't get between your legs.
You need to get this out of your head.

You should be careful.
You know I'm here to help.
He is not one to be trusted.
You are loved.
Really loved.

My life is full.
I don't need your help.
I got nothing from you when I first said bye.
I am loved.
He gives me love.

Stiff

They say hearts race,
but yours leaves no trace;
Hidden behind my bruised rib,
lies a heart so stiff;
Battered by your lies;
Churned and scorned by my half-assed goodbyes.
It stops sometimes,
with the breath inhaled when hit by your smite.
Those butterflies disappeared,
when the hollow "I Love You's" were engineered;
Created to stop the harm and calm the demon.
Why did it take me so long to see him?

They say hearts race,
when captured by love so great,
and mine did.
It nearly escaped my ribs;
So hopeful and blind ready to feel the fantasy.
Dropped from that dream of ecstasy
is where it lives now.
But stiff hearts crack and blood drowns.

They say hearts race,
from fear hidden in grace.

Please

Love just isn't in your vocabulary,
not anymore, anyway.
If so, it's misdefined;
Lost in translation;
Displayed with aggravation.
Somewhere along the way,
Love died,
scarred and petrified.
Now a fading memory;
Slowly replaced by regret;
Revealing toxicity and cowardice complacency;
But, no more;
Love is gone;
Forever lost in the past;
Glimmering with artificiality;

Give me the strength to fight;
To end the sorrow of Love lost;
To relieve my mind of his lies;
I don't care the cost.
Please tell me where to begin.
Amen.

No More

No screaming matches to prove you're right;
No silent treatment to make sure I feel your smite;

No apologies and acts of forgiveness without follow-through;
No promises waiting to be broken in a never-ending queue;

No insults used to beat me into submission;
No believing asking for help is an imposition;

No ignoring the dreams I once had;
No hiding my talent so you won't feel bad;

No tear-filled arguments I'll never win;
No controlling my gaze by lifting my chin;

No angry holes punched in walls;
No telling people "it was just a fall;"

No painful hair pulls that aren't part of the kink;
No broken glass from dishes that should've been in the sink;

No condescending conversations;
No unwarranted jealous accusations;

No threats hidden behind a smile;
No laughs to hide you're hostile;

No painfully tight grips;
No unwanted kisses forcefully placed on my lips;

No suffering through blatant disrespect;
No making excuses for your neglect;

No hand prints tattooed on my face;
No cakey make up to cover the trace;

No catering to bruises that help you feel superior;
No staying away from those who would call me a survivor;

No washing bloody clothes;
No hiding the truth that everyone already knows;

No fear of being with you behind closed doors;
No having tiffs where you keep score;

No intimacy without enthusiastic consent;
No terrible memories living in my head without paying rent;

No thinking it won't happen again;
No hoping happiness will come if I play pretend;

No thinking your temper is my fault;
No keeping the real me in a locked vault;

No pretending she doesn't exist;
No letting my valid concerns be dismissed;

No upholding vows you never wanted;
No blinding illusion that we were ever lovingly bonded;

No believing that your actions are acceptable;
No forgetting that I am more than capable;

No need to be co-dependent;
No letting you steal my financial independence;

No stopping myself from leaving;
No thinking love is more important than breathing;

No closing the blinds so nobody sees,
how awful you are to me.

Dot Dot Dot

You know I think that . . .
Maybe this isn't working
Maybe we should . . .
I'm just saying I saw you with her
. . .
I followed you . . .
Don't . . . Stop . . . That hurts
It's okay, baby, I made you angry
. . .
I realize this isn't working
I think we . . .
Because we need to talk about it
You don't want me anymore . . .
I saw the pictures . . .
OW . . . my hair . . . That hurts
It's okay, baby, I shouldn't be snooping
. . .
We're not working
Put your fist down
NO, I am speaking now!
I know about the baby
Wow . . .
Put the knife down . . .
Don't come any closer
But . . . Baby . . . I love you
Please . . . Don't . . . I . . .

OK

OK.
Pause.
Take a second.
Inhale.

Look,
you were beautiful.
You approached and took my breath away.
I lost my mind with you by my side.
You were sweet with nerves you couldn't downplay.
I heard you mumble something about being stupid.
Were you talking about me?

Love struck us,
maybe a little too strong,
but it hit us hard.
When our lips touched,
I could feel a spark,
but, when I got between your legs
there was nothing to brag about.
And, yet, I felt your love was mine.

Still, I needed a moment,
away from your gaze.
You're just so intense,
using words of love when I couldn't say the same.
It was all too much,
so I fucked around,
but, the loose aren't loyal,
and you are.

I called you mine,
and we said I do.

Did the whole charade,
loved you like a man does.
Still, you complain.
So I did as my pops taught,
and shut you up like he did Momma,
but I felt terrible.
Bought you flowers and said I'm sorry.
Still, you changed.
You weren't acting the same.

With you,
it became mundane.
The spark was gone.
You made so many mistakes.
So, I went elsewhere for love.
You put me through a lot,
and I deserved a break.

I just needed to cool off;
Took some cash and played some games;
Tried to forget how you defied me.
I came home to you most nights,
But you're just so whiny.

I buy you clothes, makeup, and give you money.
So, it came from your purse,
I gave most of it back.
Made sure you looked like something worth bragging about;
Made sure you covered the lessons you forced me to handout.
But you just wanted to make things worse.

You started getting bolder,
disrespectful, even.
After all I did for you;
After everything we've gone through?
That's fucked up!

So, I put you in your place,
like Pops said men do.

You started asking questions,
and invading my space.
Mentioning her,
like she's worth your attention.
Now, you're talking about leaving;
Thinking you're so much better;
So much smarter than me.
Who do you think you are?

I gave you love when it was hard;
Laid by your side when I could;
Made you worth it.
I'm the only one who loves you;
Just me,
But, you want to leave?
Fuck you!
You were never anything special, anyway.
Shit,
You were barely OK!

Okay

Okay.
Pause.
Take a second.
Inhale.

Here I am standing in the room,
where we danced;
Sweet moments leaving me entranced,
in the lie that is you.
Graduated from a fist to a knife;
I did say I'd spend the rest of my life,
with you.
Why'd I say I do?
This is absurd.
How did I get here?
Was this something I engineered?

I was ambitious,
ready to take on the world.
I've fallen for this scam before,
pretty-eyed sweet-talker,
only to be left behind.
To fall again is preposterous,
but meeting you my heart twirled,
I could feel it in my core;
Angelic voice and filled with laughter;
I needed to make you mine.

I thought it was love,
But, I can't even call it lust.
The future I saw when we met,
is nothing but a spec,

in the maze of my mind.
It became too much,
to hide your truth with my shallow lies.

I began to question the inconsistencies.
Were you holding my hand to show affection,
or keep me from running?
Running your hands through my hair to show kindness,
or keeping your grip on the reins?
Was I wearing make-up to feel beautiful,
or to keep you from straying?
Wearing skin-tight clothes to feel confident,
or to cage my fears in tighter?

When good intentions lead to interventions,
and my misguided affection had no real connection,
where do I stand?
What do I call myself?
Who have I become?

Confronting you about her,
who knows what will occur?
Is this my end?
In this breath I can pretend,
I'm not scared.
To be safe I tell you I still care;
Old habits.

When the exhale leaves my lips,
the knife will pierce my skin,
as you stab my heart,
my dreams will have officially fallen apart.
A victim, hopefully in the sky,
with nothing to be remembered by.
Just an angel with lips as red as the blood you made me bleed;
We'll see.

Or

When the exhale leaves my lips,
the knife will miss my skin.
I would know in my heart,
it's time for us to be apart.
I will officially say goodbye.
Confidence will grow, I'll have no reason to cry.
In life and love I will do everything to succeed,
You'll see.

One way or another I will escape.
I will be safe;
Away from you and your demon;
Away from the person I became.
Sadly, it took too long to comprehend,
but, its time to exhale,
knowing somehow,
someway,
everything will be okay in the end.

Resources for Help and Support

If you or someone you know is a victim of domestic violence or abuse, help is available.

For help, you can contact RAINN or the Crisis Text Line.

- Visit RAINN.org or call the National Sexual Assault Hotline at 1-800-656-HOPE (4673) for
- free and confidential support, available 24/7.
- Crisis Text Line
- Text HOME to 741741 to connect with a trained crisis counselor. Support is available 24/7 for any crisis.

Without the following people, this book, my dream, would have never become a reality.

Judith E. Chanza

Mami, you taught me what it means to be a woman and a good person. Thank you for paving the way and showing, by example, how to be a strong woman.

Ehimar Chanza

Papi, I wouldn't have had the courage to pursue this creative path without you. You taught me not just to speak my mind but to scream it loud enough that others don't have a choice but to listen. Thank you for encouraging me to use my words as my superpower.

Wilmaris M. Chanza

This book wouldn't be what it is without you answering all my random questions about victims and relationship dynamics to make this book as authentic as possible. I couldn't be more grateful for your support.

Carlos E. Chanza

You the best, bro! Thanks for hyping me up every step of the way.

George R. Alvarez

Love, you supported me through all the tiny little details. You helped me talk through minuscule things like comparing a comma or a semi-colon and the impact of a single word change in line – all things you don't know much about and wouldn't usually care about – but you attentively listened to me rant and spent time researching with me until I made a decision. You reminded me to take breaks, eat, sleep, relax, and have fun. Thank you for being my partner during this journey.

Jahleel Giles/Jay Valeyo

Jahleel, you have been my creative sparring partner for years. I cannot overstate your friendship's impact on me and my pursuit of creative storytelling. Thank you for every long phone call, lengthy text, and absurd conversation.

Jacqueline Cutler

You were the first person in the industry to take a chance on me and my abilities. Hearing you, someone with decades of experience, call me 'the real deal' meant more to me than I could ever properly articulate. Thank you for believing in me.

Everyone at AOS Publishing

You made my dream a reality, and I'll never forget it; thank you.